Michael Kindred is a freelance games inventor and educational consultant. He turned what was for many years a hobby in to a full-time occupation in 1978. For nine years, from 1978, he was a part-time member of the Southwell Diocesan Education Team. When inventing board and card games and devising some of the educational material, he works in close collaboration with the Revd. Malcolm Goldsmith.

The author has also produced educational material and books in co-operation with others, mentioned below, and has led courses on group leadership and creativity.

Michael is married to Maggie who is a training officer and supervisor for Lincolnshire social services. They have one daughter, Cathy.

Ideas marketed to date (foreign language titles in italics)

Board and Card Games: (most marketed by Waddingtons)
Cubex Playing Cards, Wordsworth, Pieces of Eight (became *El Dorado*), Four Sight, Hot Dog, Quiz Cards, My Word, *Ordleg, Mijn Woord Tegen 'T Jouwe, Demi Mot, Kreuzwort, Tocca a Te, Juego de las Palabras, Ordlek,* Gridword, Jailbreak, *Stop Tyven, Vluchtweg/En Fuite, Stoppt den Ede, Halten den Dieb/Au Voleur, Guardie e Ladri, Politi og Røvere, Pega Ladrao, Evasion,* Playmates, Caesar's Game, Animal Tracks, Pair-up Puzzles, *Les Dominos Géants,* Make-a-Snake, *Serpipon,* Wordsearch, Word Race Game, Quiz Quest Computer Games, Beeline, *Bienchen Schau!,* Old MacDonald, *Récré à la Ferme,* Manhunt, *Jagad,* Rally/Chequered Flag, Bewitched, *Forhaxad, Forhekset,* Odds On, Cops'n'Robbers, *Allo! Police?, Dem Tater auf der Spur!, Policias y Ladrones,* Snuggly Bugs, *Falsches Spiel mit Roger Rabbit, Vluchtweg - Duck Tales, Sherlock Holmes & Co.,* Cat Burglar, Ghostly Galleon, *Geister Schiff, Vaisseau Fantôme, Barbanera, Galeão Fantasma, Jolly Roger, Columbus.*

Promotional Games:
Quiz Cards via Waddingtons for Nabisco and Wrangler Heritage
My Word via Waddingtons for National Spastics Society, Cadbury's, Singapore Airlines and Gulf Air.
Game, Set and Match via Waddingtons for Robinson's Barley Water.

Consultancy Work on Games:
Dial Away for Waddingtons/British Telecom
2,000 quiz questions for Waddingtons Masterquiz
Puzzling Potholes and other puzzles for Scripture Union Magazine 'JAM'
Super Cluedo Challenge for Waddingtons

Educational Games and Material:
Industrial Relations
Alcohol — What do you know? for the Teachers' Advisory Council on Alcohol and Drug Education (TACADE)
Oil in the Modern World — Quiz Card Game for Waddingtons/British Petroleum Educational Service
Meet Me in Malaysia — Children's Project Pack for the United Society for the Propogation of the Gospel (USPG)
Read with Care — ninety minute set of exercises on media reporting — for Christian Aid as part of their Southern Africa Study Pack produced jointly with CAFOD and CIIR.
Work or What? — a study kit on work, unemployment and redundancy — with the Revd. Canon Eric Forshaw and the Revd. Malcolm Goldsmith.
Drugs — What do you know? for TACADE
ONE - an ecumenical board game specially created to mark the inauguration of the Council of Churches for Britain and Ireland (CCBI)

Books:
To Play and Pray — Twenty ideas for teachers — with the Revd. John Harris-Douglas
Four Celebrations — a teaching course on the Eucharist within the Eucharist — with the Revd. Canon Norman Todd.
Cryptic Crosswords and How to Solve Them — with Derrick Knight — to be published soon.

Tea Towel — Rule of the Road.

Once upon a group . . .

Michael Kindred

Illustrated by the author

Published by Michael Kindred

First published by Southwell Diocesan Education Committee
in 1984 and reprinted in 1985.

Revised edition: © 1987 (July) Michael Kindred
                    Reprinted *September 1987*
                              February 1988
                              August 1988
                              July 1989
                              February 1991
ISBN 0 9512552 0 7   *May 1992*
                              January 1994
                              April 1995

Obtainable from the author at: 20 Dover Street,
                                   Southwell,
                                   Notts.
                                   NG25 0EZ.

                                   Telephone: Southwell (01636) 813674

Price: £**4.50** nett
(discounts apply to 6 copies and over - please enquire).

Post and packing as follows:

No. of copies	1	2	3	4	5	6 and over
Add for p & p	50p	75p	£1.00	£1.25	£1.50	Post free

Please make cheques/P.O's payable to Michael Kindred.

Roy Allen Print Ltd., 52a Westgate, Southwell, Notts. Tel: 01636 813304

CONTENTS

Introduction 7

Part 1 — A brief look at origins of group behaviour:

My first group 11
When groups increase in size 12
Size of groups 13
Number of relationships and size of group 14

Part 2 — Setting up groups:

Purpose and contract 15
Number of meetings 16
Meeting place 17
Seating arrangements — type of chair 18
Seating arrangements — arranging the chairs 19
Physical and emotional space 20
Size of meeting place 21
Temperature 22
Fresh air 23
Lighting 24
Breaks, including refreshments 25

Part 3 — Boundaries and rules:

Punctuality — at the beginning 26
Degree of familiarity 27
Latecomers 28
Commitment 29
Confidentiality 30
Interruptions 31
Limits in general 32
Smoking 33
Punctuality — at the end 34

Part 4 — Some ways of looking at group development:

Task v. maintenance 35
Common threads running through various theories and models ... 36

Part 5 — What goes on in groups:

Choosing a seat 38
Introducing a subject 39
Your opening contribution 40
Communication and lack of it 41
Non-verbal communication 42
Opting out 43

Sensitivity ... 44
Honesty about feelings ... 45
The art of listening ... 46
Dominant behaviour ... 47
Fight or flight ... 48
Democracy v. autocracy ... 49
Bids for leadership ... 50
Co-leadership ... 51
Pairing ... 52
Sub-groups ... 53
Red herrings ... 54
Level of involvement ... 55
Subversive behaviour ... 56
Decision-making ... 57
Group norms ... 58
Barriers and defences ... 59
Hidden agendas ... 60
Hanging bits of ourselves on others ... 61
The transfer system! ... 62
Scapegoats ... 64
The group casualty ... 66
Labelling and stereotyping ... 67
Point-scoring ... 68
'Pearls of wisdom' ... 69
Over-dependence ... 70
Silences ... 71
Sexuality and sex ... 72
Waiting until the last moment ... 73

Part 6 — Endings:
Giving feedback ... 74
White elephants ... 75
Disbanding ... 76
Sometimes the party falls flat ... 77

Apology and acknowledgement ... 78

Introduction

In writing the introduction for this revised edition, I was not sure which to mention first: how the book came into being, or what its aim is. I have taken a chance on defining its purpose first hoping this will lead back naturally to its origins.

This book, then, is aimed at providing a light-hearted and amusing approach to a subject which can be quite heavy. I hope that it offers an easily digestible way of gaining insights into how groups tick, while at the same time helping to overcome some of the anxieties and doubts which can make people shy away from anything to do with groups and their workings. Even the mention of some of the in words and jargon concerning group behaviour can be enough to put some of us off for life!

I hope that by using the book you will become more aware of the kinds of things which go on in the groups to which you belong. The material is presented in a way which may appeal to those who are members of groups without any kind of designated leadership role. However, experience with the first edition has shown that those who do take on a leadership role, or who are engaged in running courses on group leadership and group dynamics, have found it very helpful. There are instances when I found it difficult to make it clear whether I am addressing a group member or a group leader. I decided not to struggle for this kind of clarity for various reasons: firstly, I didn't want to lose the spirit of the book which is essentially letting fun and learning go hand in hand; secondly, the approach which I have taken is bound to lead to a certain amount of ambiguity; thirdly, leadership is something which passes round a group from time to time and in various ways. Even if one member may have been appointed as a group's designated leader (or enabler or facilitator, to use other terms which some may feel are jargon, but which do express aspects of leadership), it is important to recognise and value other forms of leadership.

So a greater awareness of what follows can help you to become more sensitive to other people's needs and difficulties as well as your own. Sensitivity to others is certainly one of the key factors in developing and maintaining helpful relationships within groups (as it is in the rest of life!) Your contribution to the working of the group which comes from this greater awareness and sensitivity, may thus be enhanced.

All of us belong to groups of different sizes and kinds from birth onwards: in our family or substitute family, at school, at work, in recreational pursuits, social activities and so on. We belong to some groups because we have to and we choose others. How we get on with other members affects the whole group. Each person brings with them some 'luggage' in the form of helpful and unhelpful experiences in relationships from the recent and distant past, which will in turn have an effect on their behaviour in the group.

What follows is a brief outline of some aspects of group life in pictures and cartoons, annotated with as few words as possible. Remember that behind laughter there may be a grain of truth!

Of course, pictures, cartoons and words are no substitute for the only effective way of learning how groups tick: that is, by belonging to groups of different kinds, either as a member or leader and by taking part in competently-led courses on group work.

I am a little embarrassed by the 'Toad of Toad Hall' nature of this book, so it may help to dispel this somewhat for me, and may put you in the picture a bit more, if I tell you how the book came into being. Several years ago, my wife and I led a course on group leadership under the auspices of the Southwell Diocesan Education Committee, and during it I began to feel that there was room for a book about working in groups which was fun while having a serious purpose, to complement the very good but more academic approach of other books on the subject. I drafted it out and the Education Committee agreed to fund a trial print run in a duplicated format to see how the concept would be received. This sold well throughout the country even though we did little in the way of publicity, and it led to a reprint in 1985. This sold out in even less time. The diocese then had regretfully to say no to a more ambitious printed edition as they realised it was not appropriate for them to take on a serious publishing role. While the book had been selling I had been approaching the kinds of publishers whom I thought may have been interested. After trying about forty with no success, but getting very encouraging comments from some of them, I decided to have a go at publishing it myself. It seemed that the approach taken by the book was sufficiently out of the mainstream to be considered too risky a venture at a time when publishers were having to be very careful about economic viability.

Whilst all this was going on, a number of encouraging reviews began to appear in various papers and magazines, and I had some very complimentary letters and remarks from users of the book, together with helpful criticisms and suggestions.

I have incorporated some of these suggestions in this revised edition — but not all, as I felt that some, though in themselves valuable, would have changed the nature of the book too much. In the final analysis, I decided that it had started out as a mongrel, and a mongrel it ought to continue! It certainly was difficult at times to know what to include and what to leave out. When have you put your last brush stroke on the canvas? Anyway, I hope that what it lacks in theoretical meat in some respects, it makes up for in the ways in which it gives easily remembered pegs on which to hang future learning.

It is seemed a good idea to give some kind of ordered list of contents to help people in referring to a particular illustration or piece of text. It will be obvious that a few arbitrary decisions had to be made because some topics fall into more than one section.

Whilst the material in this book applies to groups within my own culture, I recognise that it may not offer a specific perspective towards other cultures. I would be interested to hear from anyone who has any experience of trans-cultural group work.

The birth pangs of producing the first edition and this revised one were greatly eased — as I acknowledged before — by the advice and encouragement of my wife, Maggie. I have also had an enormous amount of help from many people at various times in my life which is reflected in the way the material has come together. It may seem strange to say it, but I am glad that they are too numerous to mention! However, I feel it is worth sharing the fact that I have had several years of psychotherapy with a Jungian analyst, which, apart from marrying Maggie, was the greatest investment I ever made!

Anyway, have fun using this book. Take the issues raised seriously, but don't take yourself too seriously.

Michael Kindred.

The first group to which most people belong is some kind of family or substitute family.

The ways in which mother, father and child, or children, get on together — or fail to get on together — affect each member of that family deeply. The ones likely to benefit or suffer most are the children.

The ties and tensions may or may not be more complex where one-parent families are concerned, where substitute parents are involved, or where a child is fostered or adopted.

Our experiences in this first basic family unit will affect how we react and behave in groups to which we belong later on.

Think about recent experiences in a group. Were you reacting or behaving or feeling . . . . .

. . . . a bit like your mother or father or substitute parent used to in a similar situation?

. . . . a bit like you used to as a child?

One day, my first group . . .

. . . seemed too big

Jealousy involves two or more other people directly. We feel we want to be included in something which is going on between them, but we are at present excluded. In wanting to 'get in on the act', we may feel like getting rid of the unwanted person or persons in order to make it a cosy 'twosome'. Envy involves people indirectly. Someone else has some possession, or ability, or attribute which we would like very much, and our feelings get out of proportion.
Think back to times when you were jealous or envious in a group.
Did those feelings have their origins in your early family life?

Some groups...

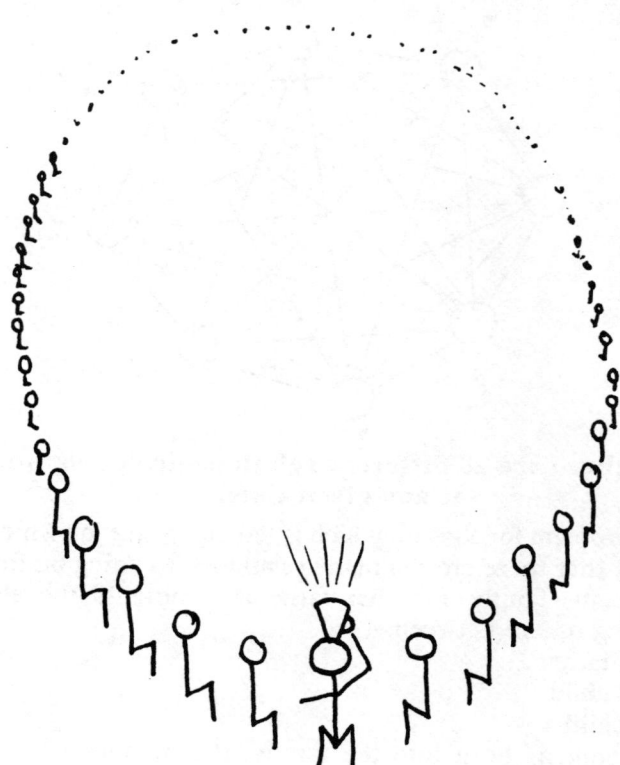

...may be too large for their purpose

Some people are 'only ones'. Others were born into large families.
Whatever your position in the family, you would have feelings about it, just as you would have feeling about any increase in the size of your family. Any such increase would affect how things were done, how present members felt about the new member, and vice versa.
These past experiences may affect how you feel about the size of groups to which you belong now.
Have you been in any groups where 'too many cooks spoiled the broth'? On the other hand, have you ever wished there were 'many hands to make light work'?
Many groups are too big for the job they have to do.

In a group of only 8 people . . .

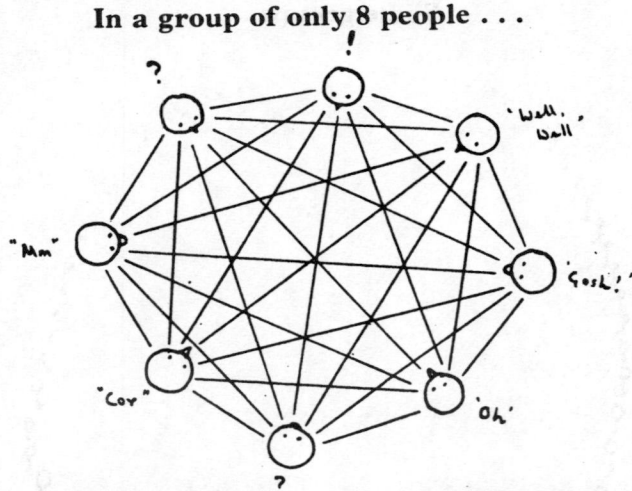

. . . there are 28 different relationships going on at any given time!

Part of the problem for a group which is too big for the job which it has set out to do, is that there are too many relationships going on for comfort. For example, in a family of mother, father and one child, the relationships that are going on are between:—

mother and father
mother and child
father and child

If another child is born into the family, the number of relationships increase to those between:—

mother and father
mother and older child
mother and younger child
father and older child
father and younger child
older child and younger child

Add one to a group of three and you've doubled the number of relationships with which members have to deal.

N.B. If you want to work out how many relationships are going on in other sizes of group, do the following sum:—

$$\frac{(\text{number in group}) \times (\text{number in group less one})}{2}$$

E.g. for a class of 30 children plus a teacher, the number of relationships is:— $\frac{31 \times 30}{2} = 465!$

Members should be clear . . .

. . . about the main purpose of the group

Think about groups to which you have belonged. In each one, did the leader . . .
 . . . state clearly its purpose in the written, (or spoken), invitation to join?
 . . . give members the opportunity, at the first meeting, to say what were their expectations?
 . . . offer the chance to see whether or not these expectations were realistic?
 . . . discuss with members whether or not they understood the purpose of the group, and whether or not they agreed with it?
 . . . make opportunities during the life of the group for evaluation of how the purpose was being fulfilled?

The more times you answer 'No' to the above, the higher the likelihood of genuine discontent in a group.

Not everyone likes marathons

Have you ever been put off by the number of meetings planned for a group?

Perhaps you have gone to the first few sessions and then realised that a certain crispness is lacking and that the task has been spread over far too long a time.

There is, of course, the other side of the coin. Have you sometimes felt that too much was being crammed into the time allotted?

The number of sessions planned for a group needs to be in keeping with the task to be accomplished.

Where you meet is important.

If you meet in one particular member's house all the time . . . .

. . . then you may find a few jealousies creeping in

(Neutral territories are sometimes best)

I expect that you have been in groups which have gone badly while meeting in the nicest of rooms.
On the other hand, you have probably met in the most unwelcoming of places, and yet been thrilled by what happened in the group.
It depends to a large extent on the people.
However, what the meeting place is like usually matters more than people think. Warmth, comfort, acceptable lighting level, adequate space, are all important.

If at all possible, it's not a bad idea...

...to have similar kinds of chairs for everybody.

There are, of course, situations where this is virtually impossible such as meeting in someone's home. It is also important to realise that some people may need a chair of a certain kind due to difficulties such as backache or arthritis.

Having said this, if all the chairs are not the same, be aware of how a certain kind of chair can influence the contribution of the person in it.
For example...

... the person who has cornered the only armchair, when everyone else is on a hardback chair, may use it quietly to opt out of the proceedings, or to feel somewhat superior, or to take a smug as well as a snug view of things.

... the person on the only stool may feel left out, or more uncomfortable than the others, or, literally, on edge!

Again, the kind of chair used is important, although in a lot of cases it's Hobson's Choice. I once went to a meeting held in a school for infants, where we had to sit on incredibly small chairs for what seemed ages. It could have been described as an overflow meeting!

Have you been in small groups where the chairs were arranged so that you couldn't see everybody's face?
Have you been in larger groups and meetings where you couldn't see most people's faces?
In either case, how far did you feel part of what was happening?
How many times have you chosen to sit on the back row if you were not all that interested in going in the first place!

In particular...

How the chairs are arranged *does* matter!

Holy — or unholy — huddles can frighten the life out of someone who likes a bit of space for themselves.

...don't sit on top of each other

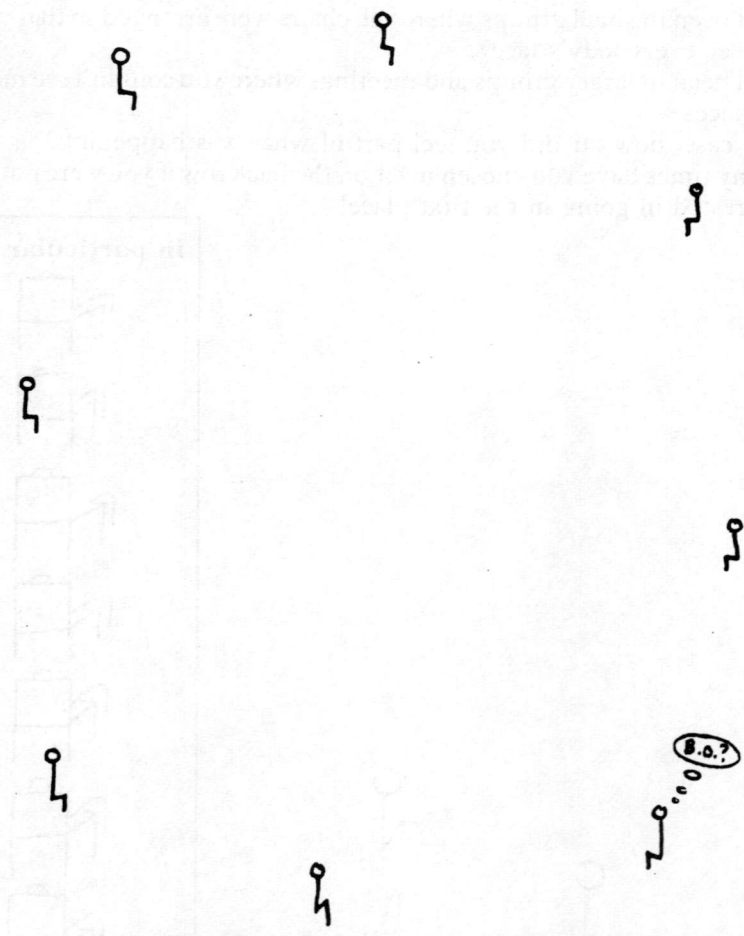

People need physical space as well as emotional space.

Have you ever felt you were sitting too close together in a group?

Or too far apart?

What is too close for you may not be close enough for someone else!

It is interesting to see the ways in which people knowingly or unknowingly adjust the space between themselves and those next to them.

Think about groups to which you have belonged. How would you have spaced the chairs?

```
Some
                    rooms
    may
           be
                         a


bit                              too



               big
                    for
                          your
      size
             of
                  group
```

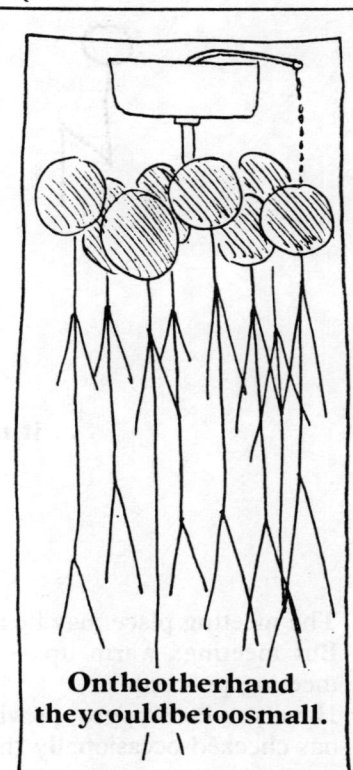

Have you ever met as the only small group in one corner of a large hall?

Some people can feel quite lost in that sort of situation.

Or have you suffered from claustrophobia and felt that feeling included has its limits?

The size of the place chosen for a meeting is important.

Ontheotherhand theycouldbetoosmall.

Getting the right temperature for the room is important...

... it may also be difficult!

The meeting place may be at an agreeable temperature at the beginning. But meetings warm up — physically as well as emotionally — as the meeting proceeds.

Have you been in groups where you have been pleased because the leader has checked occasionally that everyone is comfortable?

There are other ways of getting some ....

.... oxygen!

Ventilating a room to suit all tastes can sometimes be a problem. Some outdoor types would probably like to fling all the doors and windows wide open, while others may feel like fitting draught excluder strips during the coffee break.
A healthy stream of fresh air through an open window can turn one person's position into pneumonia corner. On the other hand the 'sealed capsule' syndrome can turn some members a whiter shade of pale.
Perhaps you have welcomed those times where the leader 'aired' the problem, so speak and tried to help everyone to feel reasonably comfortable.

Is the level of lighting more suited to . . .

. . . interrogations or developing films?

How often have you been in groups where the level of lighting has been given little consideration by the organisers or leaders?
It is something that deserves more attention than it usually gets.
The level of lighting can create moods and atmospheres ranging from restful to seductive to dramatic to intense. Our experiences in groups can be enhanced if adequate thought is given to it.

If you decide to have a coffee break...

... make sure it doesn't go on too long.

You have probably found it helpful when you have been offered one or more short breaks, (depending on the length of the meeting).
Such breaks, one of which may include refreshments, give everyone a legitimate chance to stretch, yawn and change position as necessary.
Sitting on a hard chair for a long time can distract even the most interested member.
Also, the attention span of most people is less than we imagine.

It is helpful . . .

. . . if the group starts on time.

It can be frustrating, for those who have taken care to arrive on time, to wait for others who are avoidably late.
Some people are unavoidably late at times.
Therefore, it is important that groups or meetings start at the time stated, or else the number of latecomers is likely to increase, and dissatisfaction will grow among those who continue to arrive on time.

How would you like people to refer to you in the group?

Have you been in a group where you have been addressed in a way which made you feel slightly uncomfortable or embarrassed?
It is helpful for people to have a chance to say how they would like to be known.
Some people called Michael don't like being called 'Mick' because it's a brand of dog food!

Some people find it a bit difficult . . .

. . . to come in when they're late

People arrive late for a variety of reasons. Some may have been genuinely delayed; some are in two minds about coming; some like to make a dramatic entrance to gain the attention of the group; some may be afraid of being first and misjudge their timing.

Some people, realising they are late, may find it very difficult to knock and enter. They are usually helped by the knowledge that they will be able to come in with a minimum of fuss. Have you ever been in groups where the leader has offered a word of welcome and made sure that a seat was available, and then continued with what the group was doing? In this way the feelings of all concerned were probably considered in as fair a manner as possible.

You may also have been in groups where the leader has created too long an interruption by trying to give the latecomer an account of what has happened so far, sometimes interspersed with that person's embarrassed account of why they were late. You and other members may have found this rather frustrating. An alternative course is to explain briefly to the latecomer that they can be helped to catch up later.

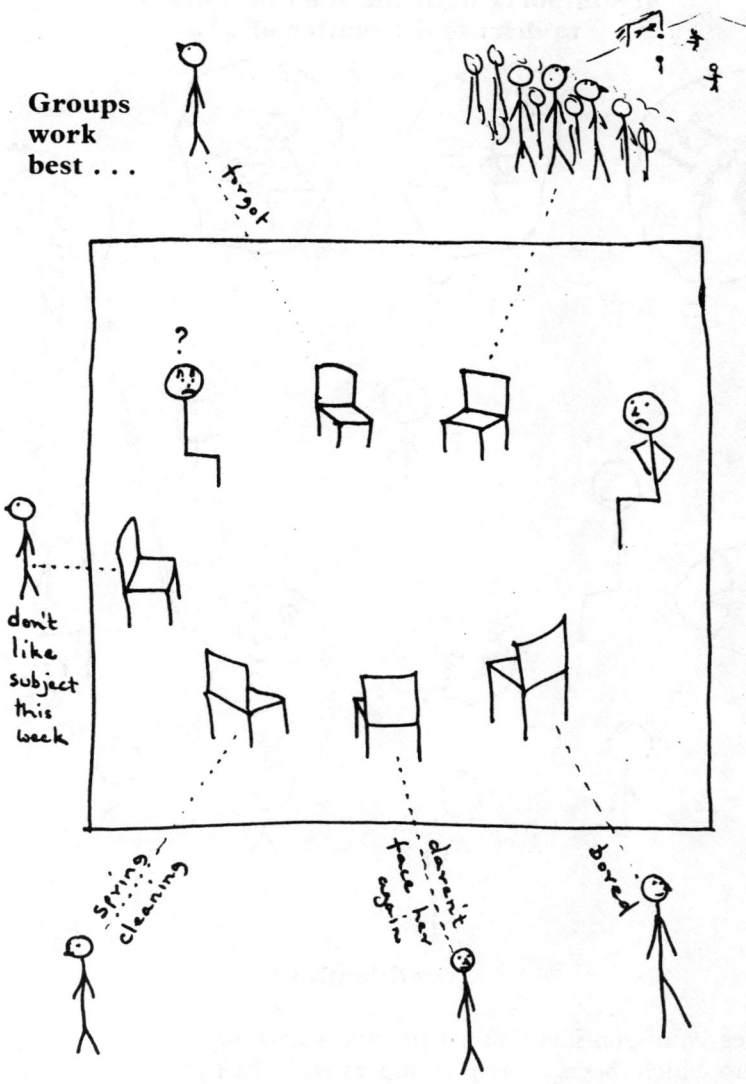

Groups work best . . .

. . . if the membership is stable

If you say that you are going to join a group which is to have a series of meetings, it is important that you take this commitment seriously. Nothing is more dispiriting to the leader and the regular members than spasmodic attendance.

It's important, at the start of a group, to discuss the matter of ...

... confidentiality

The degree of confidentiality will vary according to the type of group. A group which meets to help members with their personal problems will demand a very high degree of confidentiality.

Unless members feel that safeguard, how will they be able to share some of what is troubling them?

Some leaders fail to find an adequate consultant who is outside the membership of the group. They can find themselves needing to talk to inappropriate people for support. It is amazing how things can get back to their source.

Sometimes there may be . . .

. . . the odd interruption

Have you had experiences where the leader of a group has constantly broken off to answer the door, phone or family enquiry?

Did you feel that he or she was not really interested in the group and what it was doing?

You may find it helpful . . .

. . . to have a few boundaries and limits defined

These boundaries and limits apply to what members do **in** the group — what they do outside the group is their own affair.

Sometimes personal agendas need to be looked at. A personal agenda is that which a person knowingly or unknowingly brings to a group from his/her recent or past life outside the group, and which to a greater or lesser degree gets in the way of what the group as a whole is supposed to be doing. We all have personal agendas and with a little insight and help we can make sure that their effect on the life of the group is minimal.

If there seem to be particular personal agendas which are affecting the life of the group, there should be some encouragement from the leader for these to be acknowledged and discussed so that their effect on the group is minimised.

It is worth mentioning that, especially in discussion-type groups, some members will stray from the straight and narrow and talk about anything but the subject in hand. Leaders can sometimes have a hard job in keeping them to the point. Those who have come to the meeting understanding its purpose and are trying to fulfil it, may feel annoyed and frustrated.

Er . . . er . . .

. . . does anyone mind if I don't smoke?

The question of whether members may smoke or not should be dealt with at the first meeting.
Some non-smokers find it quite difficult to respond honestly to someone asking 'Do you mind if I smoke?', and may say 'No' in order to avoid having to cope with potentially uncomfortable feelings.
This can lead to suppressed resentment and can hinder the development of helpful relationships.
On the other hand, some smokers find it equally difficult to ask the question, knowing that some people don't like smoky atmospheres, and they too, may sit through sessions with a growing resentment.
Either way, it is good to air the subject at the beginning.

It is helpful . . .

. . . to finish sessions on time

Nothing is more annoying to most people than meetings which go on and on past their allotted finishing time.
Part of defining boundaries and limits is concerned with beginning and ending sessions.
Finishing meetings on time helps to prevent boredom, yawns, rebellions and walk-outs, also reduced membership.

Task v. Maintenance

Everything which takes place in a group is referred to as the process. This process comprises two distinct but interdependent functions: the task and the maintenance.
The task is that which the group comes together to achieve.
The maintenance is the building up and nurturing of the relationships between all the members of the group.
If the task is concentrated upon at the expense of maintaining relationships in the group, then the co-operation necessary for completing the task will deteriorate, and so the task will not be completed satisfactorily.
If the maintenance of relationships is concentrated on at the expense of the task, then again, the completion of the task suffers setbacks.
Therefore it follows that task and maintenance need to go hand in hand, and although the degree to which either is attended to at any given time will vary, they should always be complementary the one to the other.

There are various theories and models of how a group develops during its life. A brief outline follows of what seems fairly common to all these theories and models, showing that three basic phenomena tend to occur and recur:

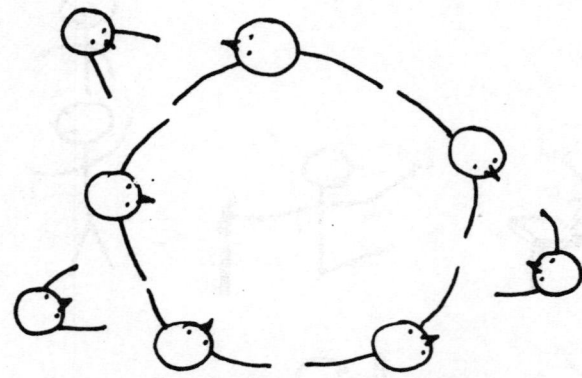

A: 'Please let me in!'

At the beginning of the group life members feel it is important to establish their position. The natural desire to feel needed and accepted and included is very prominent, although different members will show these desires in different ways.

B: 'The winner!'

At one or more points during the group life there will be bids for control, often directed at the designated leadership. Once again those doing the bidding will adopt different ways of trying to establish who is in control, varying from an open and frank attack on, or defence of, the designated leader, to more subtle ploys such as quietly manipulating others into liking the way you perform in the group!

C: Affection and disaffection

As the group progresses, members demonstrate different kinds of feelings for each other. Feelings between any two members can alter during the life of the group, so that what started out as antagonism could turn into affection, or vice versa.

These three phenomena:—
A: needing to feel accepted
B: the desire for control
C: developing feelings about other members
          continue to appear in varying proportions during the life of a group, even though at different stages one may seem more apparent than the other two.

Some people who are anxious about being in a group . . .

. . . may prefer the seat nearest the door

If you are one of the first to walk into the room where the group is meeting, how do you choose your seat?
Next to the leader — (if he or she is already seated) — does this give you a feeling of kinship with the leader, does it make you feel more secure and allay some of your anxieties?
Opposite the leader — are you preparing to do battle?
Nearest the door — do you favour flight instead of fight?
Do you find it difficult to take the last seat if everyone else has arrived before you?

There are other ways...

...of introducing a subject

How many times have you been in groups where the subject matter was introduced by a straight talk from notes? Perhaps you would have been more interested if one of the following had been used:

slides and/or a tape
role play — e.g. where members are given a particular situation and asked to act out how they would respond to it.
learning exercise — e.g. where members are asked to perform a particular task and then helped to discuss how and what they learned.
educational game — e.g. a game like Monopoly can be played as such if people are asked afterwards things like what criteria they used to make decisions and how they felt about other players.
quiz
passage from a book
reaction to pictures or advertisements
simulation — e.g. players enter into situations such as trading, setting up a workplace, producing a newspaper, and so on, and discuss at the end how they reacted to other players and to what was required of them during the simulation.

If
 you
  dive
   in
    with
     a
      big
       splash
        straight
         away . . .

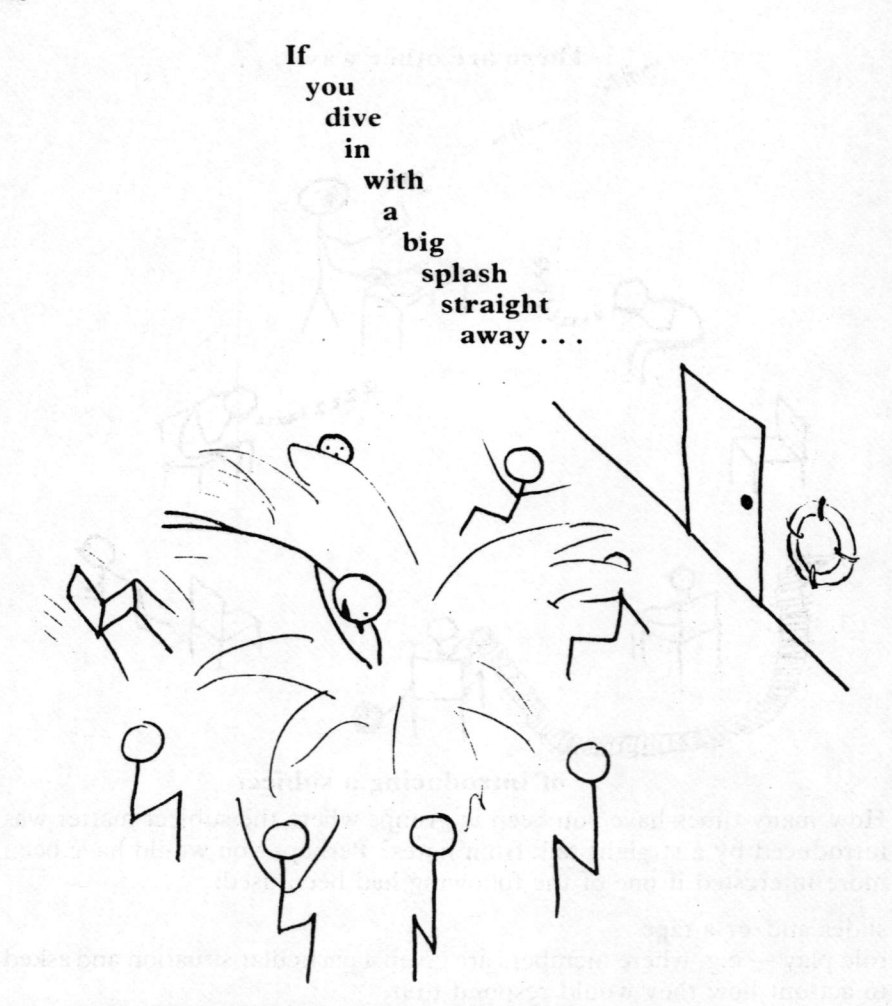

. . . the leader may throw the odd lifebelt

. . . but *you* have to learn to swim.

Anxiety is usually largely responsible for the way in which some people make a big contribution in the opening sessions of a group.
They 'dive right in' so to speak, and say things which they may regret later on. It is usually difficult for them to go back on what they said — they are afraid of losing face.
A competent leader may be able to help them through the difficulty to some extent, but the diver has to take responsibility for the splash!

People find different ways...

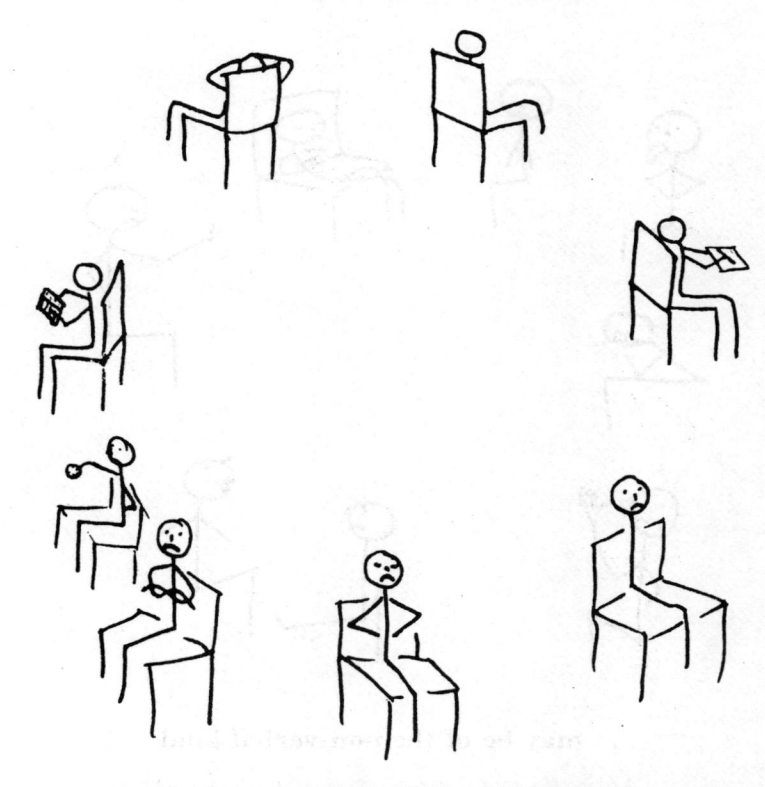

...of not communicating with each other

Various things happen in the relationships within a group which cause breakdowns in communication.
The signs of these breakdowns vary from the very obvious to those which could go unnoticed.
Someone may deliberately ignore what another person is saying, and almost interrupt them, changing the subject at the same time.
Another person may be upset by what has just happened between themselves and another member, and avoid eye contact for the rest of the session.
Whatever the signs are, it is helpful to be able to spot them, because we may be able to help someone who has received the worst of an 'exchange' and is feeling somewhat defeated.

Sometimes, communication in a group . . .

. . . may be of the non-verbal kind

We are so used to communication being by words, spoken or printed, that we sometimes forget that a great deal of what we communicate to others is done through:

facial expression
posture
specific movements of fingers, hands, legs (gestures)
skin (blushing, sweating)
laughter
crying

It is a sad fact that most of us are not very good at listening to what others are saying — we are usually more interested in what *we* want to say. When it comes to being aware of the things which are not being put into words, again, most of us could do with some training.

Be sensitive to anyone who may be opting out almost un-noticed . . .

Some people may become so worried or anxious or threatened or frightened by what is happening in a group that they will find ways of opting out.
They may remain unusually silent for long periods.
They may twist in their chair so as to try not to look at the group, or at a specific member of the group.
They may engage in pairing so that they feel safer.
They may make a lot of jokes about what is going on in an attempt to defuse the threatening situation.
A good leader will notice these signs and will try to help the person to feel a welcome part of the group again.
Leaving the room is often a cry for help or attention rather than a real wish to leave.

Be sensitive . . .

. . . to other people's feelings

In your anxiety to cope with your own feelings, you may ride roughshod over other people's at times. Try to remember that every member of the group has his or her vulnerable areas, a tenderness which once hurt may take some healing.

The paradox is that your strength may lie in behaving and reacting in a way which apparently strong people would dismiss as being weak!

So, what does it mean to be strong? Does it mean enforcing your will on others, keeping a stiff upper lip, bottling things up?

What does it mean to be weak? Does it mean sharing the fact that you are afraid of speaking in groups, that you are worried about being 'sat upon', that you find authority figures daunting?

What a lot of people count as strength is usually only a show used to cover up deeper insecurity.

What a lot of people count as weakness is usually evidence of the humanity of us all — how prone we are to make mistakes, to get things wrong, to fail to see what is in front of our noses! Admitting some of these things is normally a sign of strength of character.

Some people are very honest when it comes to feelings . . .

. . . other people's, of course!

Try to imagine what you are about to say to someone in the group, being said by them to you.
How would you feel?
If you think you would feel all right, have you had more help than they may have had in developing insight into understanding oneself and others?
If you don't know, or aren't sure, then err on the safe side!

The art of listening . . .

. . . may also apply to what is not being said

A child once defined 'listening' as 'wanting to hear'.
There is an art to listening. It involves really wanting to hear what another person is saying.
There is also an art to 'listening between the lines', to pick up what is not being said.
Listening means more than just saying 'Yes' and 'No' in the right places.
Posture and gesture and facial expression can convey whether we are really listening or not.
We are usually so busy working out what we want to say, that we wait impatiently for someone else to finish so that we can 'put our spoke in'.

Some people — (only occasionally of course!) —

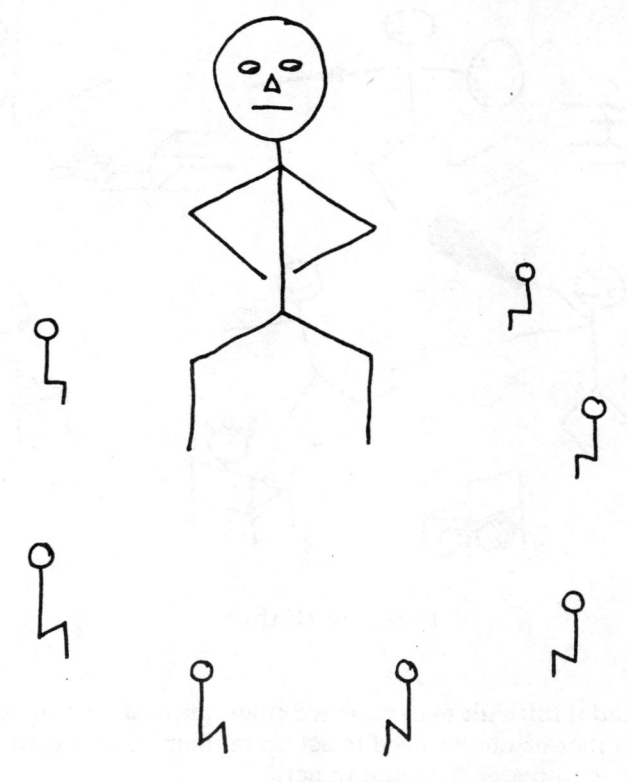

— can be a trifle dominant

A person who is unsure of himself or herself and feels insecure, may deal with these feelings in a variety of ways.

One way is to try to dominate others in order to feel less threatened by them and feel safer.

If a person is allowed to dominate the group, various things can happen — people will leave, the leader will lose co-operation from other members, the dominant person will take over the leadership, a rebellion may emerge when a few members of the group band together to 'sit on' the dominant one.

It is better if any tendancy to dominate is dealt with when it is recognised. It is helpful to deal with threatening emotions earlier rather than later. The leader should work, towards encouraging other members to help dominant personalities to take a back seat sometimes.

It is unhelpful for the leader continually to be acting as a controller while others enjoy the show and take no responsibility.

Fight or flight?

Most of us find it difficult to experience emotions **and** give ourselves time to decide whether or not we need to act upon them. Usually, the stronger the emotion, the greater the urge to act.

One example of this comes in what is generally referred to as the fight or flight response. It is very basic and necessary in the animal kingdom, and it is good that it is part of human nature too, but all too often it appears in inappropriately large doses in our relationships.

If someone in a group takes a tilt at us, do we rise up in anger and charge straight into battle, or do we turn on our heels and run like mad?

Is either course really necessary if we think about it? Would it be possible to **tell** someone how their behaviour makes us feel, with **acting** upon those feelings. For example, would it be possible to tell another member of the group that they were making you feel like hitting them, and why this was so? In this way, you are at least offering the chance of opening up some kind of dialogue, which if it is taken can lead to a building-up of a relationship rather than a breaking down or abandoning of it. On the other hand, if it is declined, you are the one who has shown some insight and inner strength. It is always more helpful to describe how another's behaviour is making **us** feel, than to condemn that behaviour.

Some group leaders are occasionally . . .

. . . less democratic than they might be

If a group leader comes over as rather autocratic at times, reactions from members will vary.

Some people enjoy being told what to do or think, and a relationship similar to that between a parent and child (appropriate enough in that setting) is maintained in an immature way between two adults, thus allowing little chance for personal growth, emotionally and spiritually.

Some people do not enjoy being told what to do or think, maybe because they are too autocratic by nature. Rebellions against the leadership will almost surely develop.

Most of us fall somewhere between these two extremes, and may find ourselves alternating in feelings about the leadership.

Sometimes there may be a bid for the leadership

If someone has set himself or herself up as a leader, then you can be sure that someone else will want to knock them down.
If a group is meeting regularly over a period, the leadership may remain uncontested for a shorter or longer time, but after that, other people may begin to feel that they could do a better job.
A competent leader will recognise these bids, and bring them out into the open to be discussed and resolved.
If the bids are ignored, then trouble is in store, because members of the group will begin to take sides and the real purpose of the group will be in danger of being forgotten.

Co-leadership...

...is not always easy!

Have you been part of a group where, instead of just one leader, there have been two acting as co-leaders?

If they haven't spent a lot of time beforehand preparing how they are going to work with each other, and getting to know each other quite well, then the group will suffer.

For example, did noticeable differences of opinion emerge between them as to how the group should be run at different stages?

Did one co-leader try to wrench all the leadership for himself or herself?

Did the other respond by:

a) doing battle?

b) giving up and becoming to all intents and purposes an aggrieved member of the group?

What is known as pairing . . .

. . . can make some people feel left out

If two people (or more) start sitting together at each session, and exchanging nods, winks or whispering confidences, then this can make others feel jealous and left out.
To make up for these feelings, other pairings can start.
The group is then on the way to disintegration in much the same way as when a sub-group has formed.
Again, the leader may bring the pairing out into the open and help members to look at the reasons for it, and the effect it is having on the group.

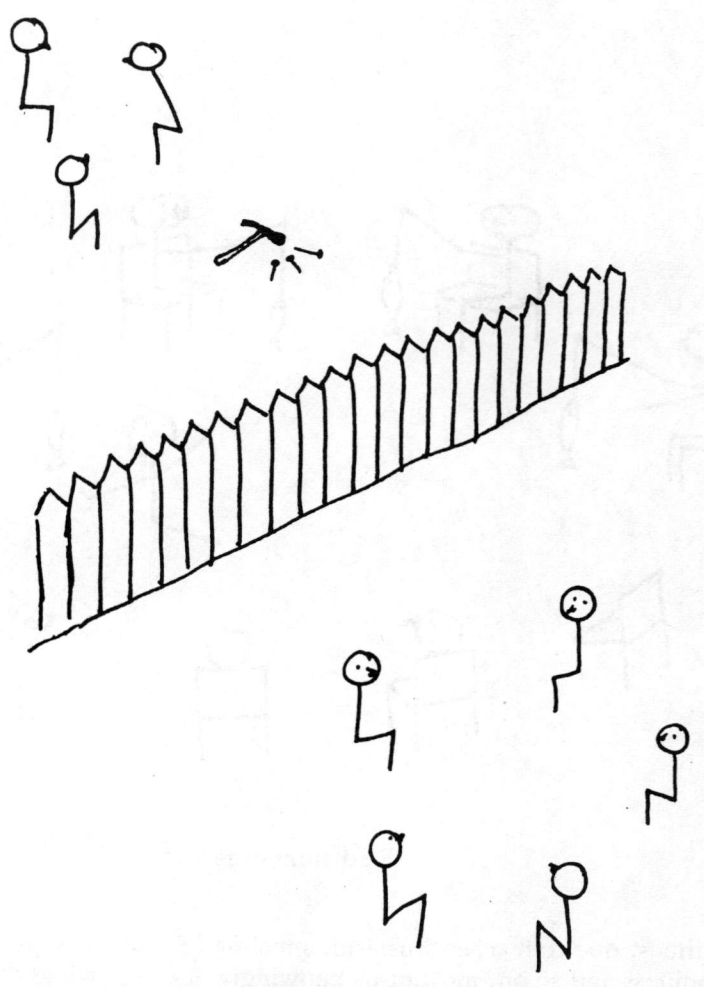

Sub-groups can form

When two or three people begin to disagree with the leader, and with others who appear to be on his or her side, then the group will fail to remain a single unit working together for a purpose, but will become two separate groups within the group.

Again, as with bids for the leadership, if this sub-grouping is not acknowledged and dealt with, the effectiveness of the group is at risk if it is a task centred group with a job to do. If the group is using the time specifically for studying itself a simple 'mirror' comment about what is going on may be the best remedy, e.g. 'I notice that there are several conversations going on at this point'.

Red herrings

At times, due to fear, enthusiasm, a feeling of insecurity, rebelliousness, happiness and so on, most of us knowingly or unknowingly deflect other members of the group from the task in hand. Some people are more accomplished deflectors than others, but we all do it to some degree: the anecdote that suddenly occurs to us, the need to change the subject quickly to avoid the 'hot potato', the story about what happened to someone outside the group, instead of what is happening to us right now.

The odd red herring here and there can be acceptable, especially if the group can be helped to see why such a deflection was used. A whole shoal unacknowledged could break the group net!

Some people get too involved

We all get involved in different ways and at different levels with any group to which we belong.
The involvement can be practical, intellectual, emotional or spiritual — in any combination.
It will vary at different stages during the life of the group.
Sometimes it will vary almost from minute to minute.
The reasons for getting involved are numerous — they include:—
interest
excitement
curiosity
some emotional need not met outside the group
pressure from one or more other members of the group
some unrecognised need which is not being met.

It is difficult to say what getting too involved means — it will vary from person to person. An example of over-involvement which could lead to difficulties would be a married person falling in love with someone in the group.

There are those of us who can be quietly subversive

The rebellious toddler and the rebellious adolescent lurk around in all of us!
Taking a tilt at authority, or at people we don't like can be quite exciting and fun — for us — it may not be quite so enjoyable for our opponents. Sometimes people will steer a course between being openly rebellious or 'awkward', and saying nothing, (thereby probably bottling up their feelings). It may emerge as a sort of 'borderline' remark where you are not sure whether they are being quietly rebellious, or whether they have put their finger on something important which is happening in the group.

There may be odd times when it's difficult to reach a decision

Someone once said that democracy is the least evil form of government. On the one hand it gives everyone a chance to influence the way the decision-making goes.

On the other hand, it can lead to a watered-down form of what may have been a very good idea.

In groups, it is important continually to evaluate the degree to which people feel free to contribute to the decision-making processes. Is anyone feeling pushed out? Is someone's opinion lightly dismissed without good reason? Is there a good level of co-operation in the group?

'Please, sir'.

All groups, like families, have their rules, often not stated, but nevertheless very powerful. These are known as group norms.
Have you noticed, in groups to which you have belonged, what rules were being adhered to? Did the leader help members to be aware of what these were and try to ensure that individual's rights were not being trampled upon?

Sometimes someone may erect the odd barrier

Right from birth, we put up all sorts of emotional defences and barriers to help us to cope with what makes us feel insecure, frightened, threatened, anxious, worried.

Sometimes, the situation which has threatened us initially, is repeated enough times for the defence to become a really hardened one.

For example, perhaps you couldn't cope with your parent's anger — so now you tend to 'pour oil on troubled waters' and 'make the peace' in any situations involving confrontation — so that people's anger is kept under — and so your anger doesn't surface.

So you may find yourself 'keeping a stiff upper lip', having a 'poker face', denying that you feel in a certain way about something when challenged, etc.

A competent group leader will be aware of the existence of these defences and help to create the kind of atmosphere where people feel less need to keep them so high.

~~Sometimes~~, well ~~quite~~ often ... ~~almost~~ always ...
Always, there are things in people's lives
outside the group which affect their contribution
in the group ...

... this is known as the hidden agenda ...
sometimes not so hidden either!

You take your emotional suitcase with you wherever you go!
Some people keep it tightly locked. Others let it spill open all over the place.
Most of us get a few things out from time to time — some are put back hastily — others the group may help us to wear for a while.
So, the things which have happened to us an hour ago, that day, that week, five years ago, in childhood, and so on, can be on our minds while the set agenda for the session is being worked through.
Some experiences will be upsetting enough to get in the way of your effective contribution to the work of the group.
That's not a criticism implying that we shouldn't let them get in the way — it is saying that we should acknowledge that this is normal for all of us, and should be recognised and acknowledged by the leader.

How do we see other members of the group?

We may project aspects of our own personality on to them at times

If I am 'big-headed' but am not aware of it, I can easily think of someone else as big-headed. I then don't have to consider whether I may have the fault of which I accuse others.

If I know that I have a cruel streak in me — and I wish I hadn't — and don't want other people to know, it is easy for me to accuse other people of being cruel. It lets me off the hook. It makes my own cruel streak seem not so bad if others are cruel too.

These kinds of 'projections' of aspects of our own personality onto others, go on in different degrees all the time in any group.

Of course, it may be the other way round. In a group we may be under some pressure to accept too readily others' views of us. The leader needs to watch for members' discomfort if this seems to be happening, as such 'introjection' is unhelpful.

If these kinds of feelings are gradually acknowledged and people make a genuine attempt to understand them, then relationships can improve. If they remain unacknowledged, relationships will continue at a shallow level and any work the group has to do will suffer accordingly.

Anyone in the group may transfer to another member feelings associated with someone they know outside the group . . .

aunt · *dad* · *mum* · *teacher* · *brother* · *lover*

"you're just like....."

. . . this can be confusing, as lots of transferences are taking place at any given moment.

Someone in the group may see you as the 'spitting image' of someone they know.

Or you may have a particular characteristic, mannerism or type of voice, which reminds them very much of someone they know (or knew).

If the person they are reminded of is 'lovely' or 'fatherly' or 'so kind' in their eyes, you may find they are seeing those same qualities in you. (Perhaps without much justification!)

If the person they are reminded of was someone 'they couldn't stand at any price', you may find that you are being ostracised by them for no real reason.

The most common 'transference' concerns a person's own mother and father. If, for example, a person really loved their own mother, and you remind them very much of their mother, you may find them more than usually affectionate towards you.

... at the
    same time
    what feelings
    associated with people
    you know outside the group ...

... now who does that person on my left remind me of?

Venus ← *Father* ← *Son*

little brother

big sister *teacher*

... are you transferring back to other members of the group?

If other people are doing this to you, what are you doing to them?
If you were afraid of your father, for example, and someone in the group has an irritating mannerism just like your father's, you may find yourself becoming afraid of the member, for no good reason.
If these transferences can gradually be acknowledged, there is a real chance that misunderstandings can be resolved to some extent, paving the way for deeper relationships within the group.

Why do we need someone...

...to be the scapegoat?

If you find difficulties are entering into a relationship, or you feel in a vague way that 'life's difficult' at present, it is easier to blame other people or circumstances, than to take any responsibility yourself.

It is so easy to see the problems of life as being 'out there', and that the difficulties are caused by other people all the time.

Of course, other people can cause us pain or anxiety and circumstances can be hard.

But that doesn't let us off the hook. We need to look at what part we are playing in any deteriorating relationship. Which problems are of our own making?

In groups, it is very easy to get another, perhaps apparently 'weaker' member of the group, to take the blame. The inner problems of the group members are put 'out there' for safety onto a 'scapegoat'.

And for safety . . .

. . . the scapegoat is sometimes located outside the group

Rather than find someone in the group to blame for our own shortcomings, it is much less threatening to blame someone, or some 'body' outside the group.

        Likely candidates are:—
        the vicar
        the church
        the state
        society
        the government
        teachers
        doctors
        God

        etc.

A competent leader will be aware of this 'running away' and will bring the focus of attention back into the group.

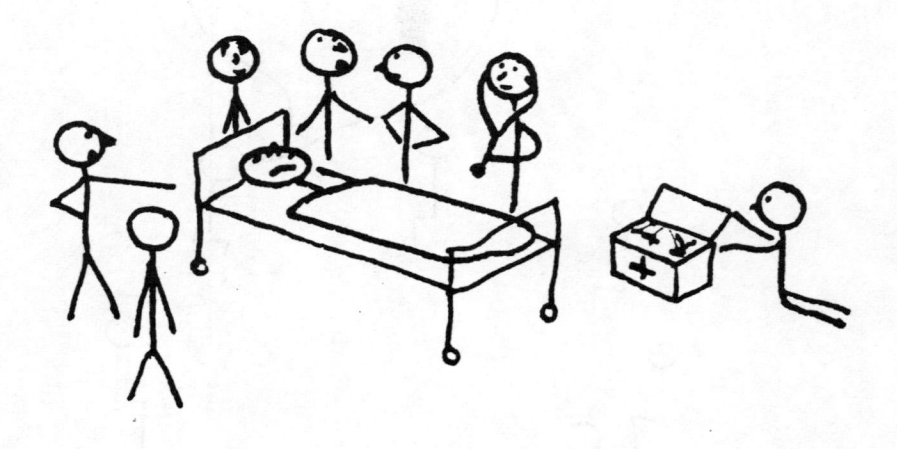

The group casualty

Have you found that sometimes one or two members of a group will initiate and encourage a 'case conference' about another member of the group who has shown some anxiety or fear or difficulty?

Soon, if the leader is not careful, everyone will become hooked on this golden opportunity to forget their own problems or the task of the group. Have you ever come under the microscope in this way? How did it feel? Some may find the sudden attention flattering initially and join in the game eagerly. Eventually, the pace may hot up as the probes go deeper, and suddenly they are desperate to locate the 'EXIT' sign. Others may immediately resent the appearance of doctors and nurses who didn't seem to be there before. Either way, it is usually a harrowing experience for the one who is the centre of this kind of attention.

Or, dare it be asked, have you ever become drawn in at the sharp end of this game of one-upmanship, and found that a certain smugness was creeping over you, accompanied perhaps by a feeling of being rather virtuous?

Labelling people . . .

. . . causes problems

A convenient way of avoiding facing up to problems — our own and other people's — is to label or stereotype them.

If we can give a name to someone's upsetting or worrying behaviour, then it somehow, seems safer; we may even be misled into thinking we have solved the matter.

It is much harder to avoid labelling people and treat them as fallible human beings like yourself.

So, in groups, where feelings of insecurity can run quite high, labelling is an easy escape from trying to discover what is really hindering the growth of a relationship.

If you want to score points off each other . . .

If your are feeling somewhat at a disadvantage in a group for some reason, one way of trying to cope with it is to do or say something which puts another member (or members) at a disadvantage.
For example, someone may have disagreed with something you said. You then wait for a chance to disagree with them.
This game of 'points scoring' can easily start in a group, and unless it is acknowledged and talked about, it can disrupt the real task of the group.

At some point, arrangements may have to be made . . .

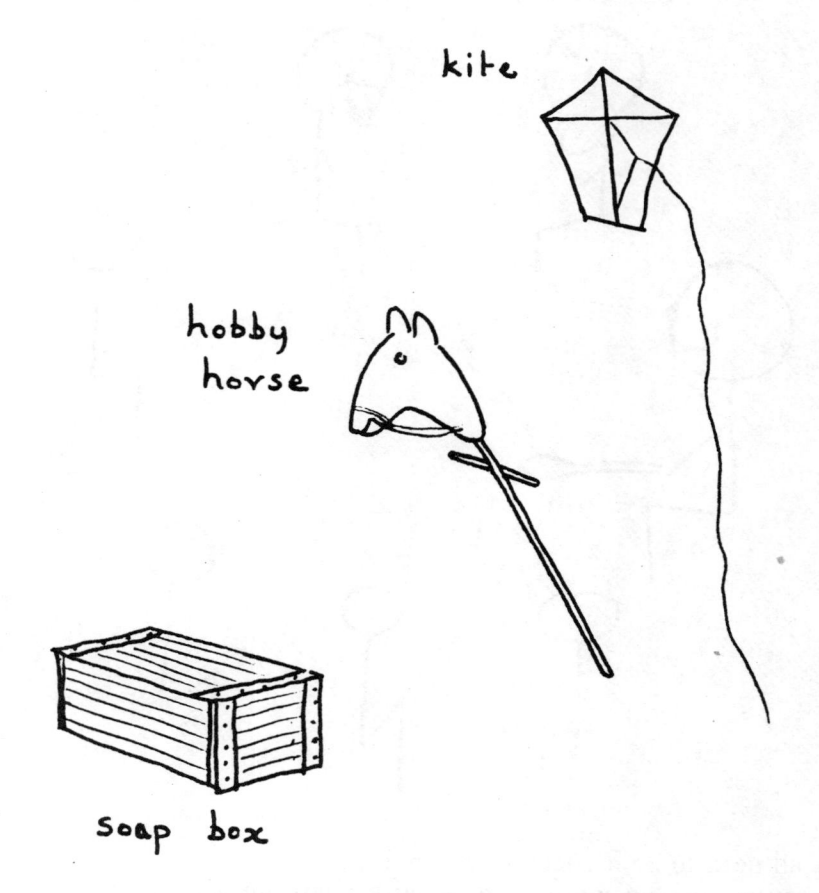

kite

hobby horse

soap box

. . . for the disposal of various pieces of equipment which are cluttering up the group space

We all have our favourite topics, opinions we love to give other people the benefit of, 'pearls of wisdom' that people are just waiting for, etc. Irrespective of what the group is supposed to be doing, some people can work the discussion round to just what they are itching to hold the floor with.
They need to be steered, firmly and with kindness, back to the point.

Occasionally... well, quite often... some group leaders can encourage over-dependence

We all need to be needed. This is normal.
Sometimes, a person's need to be needed gets out of proportion because his or her needs aren't being adequately met.
So that person strives to set up situations where they are needed by people who are in need.
Some social workers, doctors, clergy, nurses and people in the helping professions generally, fall into this category.
Some group leaders do too.
This can mean that people in the group are not allowed to 'grow up' emotionally, (rather like some men are described as still being 'mother's boys'), so the leader remains very much an immature source of wisdom, strength, help, comfort and so on.
A competent group leader allows members to grow in independence.

It is important to experience silences
(planned or not) . . .

. . . however, some members may find them difficult

Silences in groups can be experienced by some people as very threatening. They tend to want desperately to do something to break the silence, but are afraid that if they do, all eyes will turn upon them.
And yet some people can enjoy silence together and find it helpful and even moving.
So silences — planned or not — can affect members very differently.
Some people find that their anxiety is lessened if they know how long a planned silence is going to be.

For some reason...

... the subject of sex seems to be avoided

When we are in a group, (as anywhere else) there is no hiding the fact that we are either male or female, (except that some modes of dress can be misleading!).

Our essential 'maleness' or 'femaleness' is there for all to be aware of.

We are all bi-sexual, so each male will display some female characteristics and each female will display some male characteristics. The proportions vary from person to person.

The difficulties which past generations have had in discussing sexuality are around today. Some people are more inhibited than others.

Discussions about sexuality and sex will not arise in some groups because their purpose is not orientated that way, but members still need to be aware that each person present is showing a mixture of male and female characteristics. (Why are women so often on refreshments!).

People often wait until the very last moment . . .

*. . . before saying what's *really* on their mind.*

It is well known by counsellors and therapists that a client will often wait until the session has nearly ended, before telling them about something that is worrying them, or which they feel diffident about revealing.

This is usually done because the client knows that if any upsetting emotions are aroused by this late 'revelation', he or she can make a quick exit because time is up!

The same thing happens in groups and the situation needs careful handling. A leader could fall into the trap of beginning the meeting all over again, so to speak, in order to look at what has been raised and not appear dismissive. This could lead to annoyance among those who wish to leave on time.

Giving feedback

In some groups it may be appropriate for members to offer each other appraising comments to help develop their own performance. It is important, if such feedback is given, that the leader define the rules for this and set an example him/herself. Feedback is helpful if it is:
a) specific: e.g. "When you mentioned X in the group on Wednesday I found it useful."
and
b) personal: e.g. "When you keep interrupting X I feel annoyed."
Vague, impersonal statements which are not specific such as "Everyone in the group thinks X is a waste of time", are unlikely to enhance either individual members or the life of the group.
Techniques such as asking each member in turn to state something appreciated or something regretted about the group may be useful. Another possibility is for each member to think of a symbolic present they would like to give to each fellow participant. For example, someone who contributes many new ideas may be symbolically offered a computer. The presents can also provide a gentle form of feedback, so long as they are sensitively offered, e.g. a telephone for someone who does not keep in touch.

White elephants

Sometimes a person may reintroduce something which has previously arisen — they may bring the same thing up repeatedly. Such 'white elephants' are no longer really needed and are particularly noticeable towards the end of the life of a group.
For example, one member may make repeated complaints about the same thing.
The bringing in of white elephants can be an indication of the group's value rather than otherwise.

Some groups find it difficult to disband

Every group has a life of its own, and just as it was brought into being, so must it have an end.

Some groups, of course, meet for a continuing purpose and will go on year after year with changing membership.

However, most groups need a reasonable life span appropriate to their purpose. This avoids staleness, boredom and diminishing membership. If people have formed good relationships during the life of the group, it is understandable that they won't want to break up.

So it is essential that a group has a chance to anticipate the coming feelings of loss, to share them, and to help each other in coming to terms with them. A party, games and small presents can help the process (presents should be 'neutral' — i.e. not ones which make a specific point about the recipient).

Sometimes the party falls flat . . .

There are occasions when there is too much unfinished business around to allow an end-of-group party to go with a swing.

A may still be seething at something B said five meetings ago

C may be feeling hurt by a remark made by D last week

E may not have recovered from being made the group casualty two weeks ago

F may feel that s/he just missed taking over the leadership. If only there had been a few more meetings . . .

G may be cross with D for getting at C

H may be the only one free of tangles and can't understand why people aren't enjoying themselves. (But if s/he can't understand then it looks as though there is some unfinished business here as well!)

Some groups can get too academic!

This page is by way of an apology and an acknowledgement rolled into one. Normally a bibliography appears at this point in the book. I decided that it would be out of character with the rest of the book to provide such a reading list — so, my apologies to those whose hopes have been dashed! Those who still have a yen for some weightier material will, I am sure, be able to tap the resources of the appropriate bookshops and libraries.

At the same time, I want to acknowledge the indirect help I have received from those who have written about groups and their workings. This has been passed on to me by those who have made the material their own and have led courses and seminars concerned with this whole area of groupwork.